BACK IN TIME

LIVING AND WORKING IN THE
PRE-COLUMBIAN AMERICAS

Edited by
Joanne Randolph

E **Enslow Publishing**
101 W. 23rd Street
Suite 240
New York, NY 10011
USA
enslow.com

This edition published in 2018 by:
Enslow Publishing, LLC.
101 W. 23rd Street, Suite 240
New York, NY 10011

Additional materials copyright © 2018 by Enslow Publishing, LLC

Library of Congress Cataloging-in-Publication Data

Names: Randolph, Joanne, editor.
Title: Living and working in the pre-Columbian Americas / edited by Joanne Randolph.
Description: New York : Enslow Publishing, 2018. | Series: Back in time | Includes bibliographical references and index. | Audience: Grades 3-6.
Identifiers: LCCN 2017001915| ISBN 9780766089792 (library-bound) | ISBN 9780766089778 (pbk.) | ISBN 9780766089785 (6-pack)
Subjects: LCSH: Indians--History--Juvenile literature. | Indians--Social life and customs--Juvenile literature. | Indians--Antiquities.
Classification: LCC E58.4 .L58 2017 | DDC 970.004/97--dc23
LC record available at https://lccn.loc.gov/2017001915

Printed in China

To Our Readers: We have done our best to make sure all website addresses in this book were active and appropriate when we went to press. However, the author and the publisher have no control over and assume no liability for the material available on those websites or on any websites they may link to. Any comments or suggestions can be sent by email to customerservice@enslow.com.

Photo Credits: Cover, p. 1 Anton Foltin/Shutterstock.com; series logo, jeedlove/Shutterstock.com; back cover, Reinhold Leitner/Shutterstock.com; hourglass on spine, MilaLiu/Shutterstock.com; pp. 4, 11, 23, 29, 38 Vojtech Vlk; p. 5 Gary Hincks/Science Source; p. 7 Private Collection/© Look and Learn/Bridgeman Images; p. 9 Werner Forman/Universal Images Group/Getty Images; p. 10 Designua/Shutterstock.com; pp. 12, 16–17 Private Collection/Wood Ronsaville Harlin, Inc. USA/Bridgeman Images; p. 15 MPI/Archive Photos/Getty Images; p. 18 Rob Hainer/Shutterstock.com; p. 20 Werner Forman Archive/Bridgeman Images; p. 24 Private Collection/Photo © Dirk Bakker/Bridgeman Images; p. 26 Zack Frank/Shutterstock.com; p. 27 Richard A. Cooke/Corbis/Getty Images; p. 30 pavalena/Shutterstock.com; p. 32 Print Collector/Hulton Archive/Getty Images; p. 33 Diego Grandi/Shutterstock.com; p. 35 PHAS/Universal Images Group/Getty Images; p. 37 Florilegius/Science & Society Picture Library/Getty Images; p. 39 Dorling Kindersley/Getty Images; p. 40 Universal History Archive/Universal Images Group/Getty Images; pp. 42–43 Allik.

Article Credits: Evelyn Feld, "From Hunters & Gatherers to Settlers and Traders," *Cobblestone*; Peter Roop, "Following the Food," *Cobblestone*; E. Barrie Kavasch, "Ancient Mounds," *Cobblestone*; Elizabeth T. Horton, "Elegant Fabrics," *Dig Into History*; Ann Stalcup, "The Colorful History of Mexico," *Faces*; Rani Iyer, "Reconstructing Copán," *Faces*; Sylvia Whitman, "Not So Far-Fetched," *Dig Into History*.

CONTENTS

CHAPTER 1

FOLLOWING THE FOOD

T he small band of nomadic hunters hurriedly broke camp. Their leader had just returned with word of a herd of mammoths grazing beyond a line of faraway hills. Everyone in the camp—men, women, and children—carried their belongings as they set out across the rolling plains in pursuit of the mammoths. The band moved slowly eastward, following animal trails, toward the country of the rising sun. Unknowingly, these hunters were leaving Asia and entering America.

Archaeologists believe that a scene similar to this one may have happened as many as forty thousand years ago, when small groups of hunters crossed a wide land bridge between Asia and America.

Before this event, the vast continents of North and South America were uninhabited by humans. After these migrations, however, the human population spread from the frozen ice sheets of North America's Alaska all the way to the tip of South America's Tierra del Fuego.

How did those first people traverse all that way? Most scientists agree that they probably walked—a distance of nearly 10,000 miles (16,093 kilometers)! That's not so unbelievable if you consider that their migration took several thousand years. In fact, they might not even have known they were migrating. Perhaps they moved south

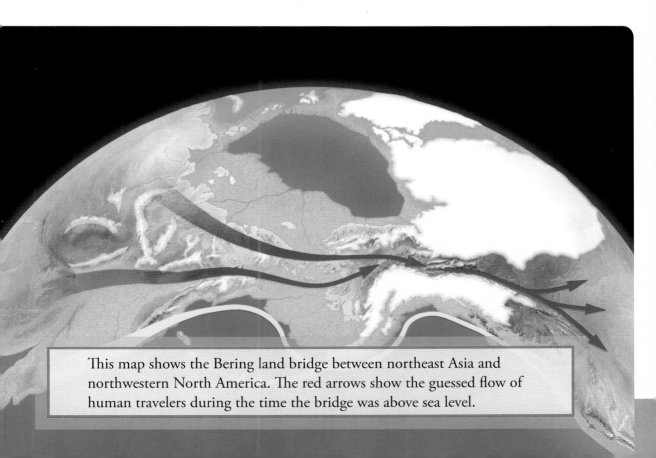

This map shows the Bering land bridge between northeast Asia and northwestern North America. The red arrows show the guessed flow of human travelers during the time the bridge was above sea level.

slowly over many generations as they followed herds of animals and looked for new sources of plant food. One scientist has used the word drifting to describe this movement. No matter what it is called, this movement was the first important migration in the history of the Americas.

Who were those first Americans? Where did they come from? What were their lives like? What land was it that they crossed in reaching America? What traces did they leave behind?

These questions have puzzled people for centuries.

PALEO-INDIANS

Archaeologists call those early nomadic hunting people Paleo-Indians, meaning "early Indians" or "old Indians." The Paleo-Indians are believed to be the ancestors of today's North, Central, and South American Indian groups. The Asian origins of the physical makeup of modern-day American Indians have been confirmed. Although Native Americans from different places look different, they share certain general features with the Mongoloid people of Asia: dark eyes, straight black hair, stockiness, similar traits in teeth, scant body hair, and brown skin color.

Archaeologists have concluded that the first Americans were skilled toolmakers, used fire, hunted large game such as mammoths, and moved about in pursuit of their prey. The first Paleo-Indians to reach America had no idea that they were entering a new, unexplored land. They simply were following the herds of mammoths, horses, camels, and musk oxen that they needed for survival. The animals provided meat for food, bones for tools and weapons, and hides for clothing and shelter. When the animals moved, so did the hunters, who ultimately trailed their wandering prey to an uninhabited continent.

Prehistoric hunters worked together using primitive tools to help them hunt and kill animals, such as this mammoth, for food.

IN SEARCH OF THE EARLIEST SITES

During the Pleistocene Ice Age (which ended about eleven thousand years ago), mile-thick glaciers covered vast parts of North America, Europe, and Asia. With so much of the earth's water frozen, ocean levels dropped low enough to expose a 1,000-mile-wide (1,609-kilometer-wide) isthmus between Asia and North America. The first humans most likely entered North America by walking across this exposed land bridge located between Siberia (part of the Russian Federation) and Alaska. Once beyond the glacier-locked lands of the Northwest, the

Paleo-Indians then spread throughout the two American continents. Over the centuries, they learned to adjust to the environments in which they settled.

When the earth experienced a warming trend and the glaciers began to melt, the land bridge, called Beringia, vanished beneath the rising waters of the Bering Strait. Archaeologists have often attempted to find sites where the earliest Americans lived, but today, 56 miles (90 km) of frigid water separate Alaska from Siberia. Since Beringia currently lies under water, archaeological investigation there is almost impossible. Many archaeologists feel that the best sites might be found either on the high ground that once overlooked the grassy plains of Beringia or in the mountain passes of Alaska. At one of these sites, Onion Portage in Alaska, archaeologists found evidence of human occupation that possibly could be fifteen thousand years old.

Another site discovered by archaeologists in the mid-1920s in Folsom, New Mexico, showed evidence of human hunters that trapped and killed Ice Age bison. These hunters were skilled stone workers who made distinctive spear points that are easily identified even today. One of these Folsom points was found between the ribs of a slaughtered bison. Because those animals have been extinct for at least ten thousand years, the presence of the spear point proved the existence of human hunters in North America at least that long ago.

The ancestors of these hunters must have arrived in North America far earlier. But no site has provided enough proof for a majority of archaeologists to agree on an exact migration date. However, new sites are being discovered and excavated, and additional knowledge is being gained all the time. One thing is certain: those roving hunters who crossed Beringia discovered the Americas many centuries before the first Europeans reached the continents' eastern shores.

Folsom points, such as this one, were fixed to the end of spears around ten thousand years ago. They got their name from where they were found by archaeologists.

CONTINENTAL DRIFT

BEFORE  **AFTER**

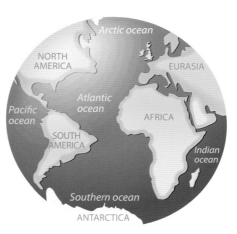

Two hundred million years ago, all the continents were one large land mass, but over time, due to forces inside Earth, they began to move apart. Eventually, they made it to the positions they are in today. But even today, the continents are moving!

SUPER CONTINENT

It is believed that millions of years ago, Earth consisted of just one giant continent, Pangaea, surrounded by a single ocean. About 250 million years ago, that massive continent began to split up, with what would become the Americas breaking off and drifting away from the future continents of Europe, Asia, and Africa.

This scientific theory was called known as continental drift, but geologists now refer to it as plate tectonics. Earth's outermost layer, the crust, is divided into large pieces called plates that glide over the mantle, the second layer, at a rate of 1 to 2 inches (2 to 5 cm) per year. Millions of years from now, the continents will look different from today.

CHAPTER 2

FROM HUNTERS & GATHERERS TO SETTLERS & TRADERS

The many groups of people that migrated across the land bridge ended up in lots of different places in the Americas, from present-day Canada down into Mexico, Central America, and South America. For a moment, we will focus on the groups that settled in the southeastern United States as an example of how the societies came about and progressed before Europeans arrived during the 1500s.

This illustration shows what the artist imagined the scene to look like as the first Clovis Paleo-Indians traveled across wide plains into North America carrying their belongings.

The earliest Indians gathered roots and berries and hunted large animals, including mastodons, giant beavers, bears, sloths, woolly rhinoceros, long-horned bison, antelope, moose, and caribou, among others. The Indians used tools and weapons made out of stone and bone.

The animals that provided these Paleo-Indians with food, skins, and tools continually moved to new areas where the climate was milder, including the Southeast. Various waves of Paleo-Indians followed these animal migrations, settling at different times. This explains the difference in the languages and customs of the descendants in this diverse Indian grouping.

There are four major language groups currently in use by Indians in the Southeast. Muskogean is spoken by the Creeks, Choctaws, Chickasaws, Seminoles, Alabamas, and Koasatis. Southeast Iroquoian is spoken by the Cherokees; Southeast Siouan by the Catawbas and Biloxis. A language possibly related to Algonquian is spoken by the Natchez. Additional Indian groups that lived in the Southeast spoke other languages that have been incompletely identified and studied by scholars. Most of these peoples, however, were killed by disease and war or absorbed by other Indian groups after the Europeans arrived in the 1500s.

CHANGE IS IN THE AIR

Between 12,000 and 10,000 BCE, temperatures in the Southeast gradually began to rise, causing larger game animals—including the mastodon, giant sloth, and long-horned bison—to become extinct. This forced the Paleo-Indians to change their diet to include smaller animals such as deer, rabbits, squirrels, and turtles. They also began to eat fish from the waters and more berries, nuts, and roots from the land.

One southeastern site from this time period has been discovered and dated by scientists at about 12,000 BCE. The Thunderbird site, found by archaeologists in Virginia's Shenandoah Valley, shows that these hunter-gatherers had settlements in which they stayed for part of the year. Soil patterns displayed traces of wooden posts belonging to a type of shelter. With these patterns as a guide, archaeologists—using stone and bone tools similar to what the Indians had at the time—were able to reconstruct a house that would have provided refuge for about thirty people.

The Windover site, near Disney World and the Kennedy Space Center in Florida, dates to between 8000 and 7000 BCE. It was discovered in 1984 by archaeologists from Florida State University, who excavated more than one hundred burial sites that contained bodies wrapped in woven cloth and grass mats. The bodies were lying beneath a covering of peat and wood. Peat, acting as a very effective preservative, allowed the contents of these sites to remain intact and thus, easy to identify. These findings indicate that the Paleo-Indians had developed and mastered many useful skills and technologies.

SETTLING DOWN

During the period between 6000 and 3000 BCE, the Paleo-Indians refined their hunting, fishing, and gathering tools. More efficient techniques let them stay in certain regions for longer periods of time, allowing them to grow familiar with the area's rivers, lakes, land, trees, plants, animals, fish, birds, and weather patterns. Scholars believe that these early Indians, who already had a natural abundance of food in the river valleys, remained in permanent settlements long before they developed farming as a source for their food supply.

By 2000 BCE, these ancestors of modern American Indian tribes had begun to cultivate and domesticate plants such as sunflowers, goosefoot, knotweed, maygrass, barley, and marsh

As the first people in North America grew more advanced, they came up with new tools for catching food. These Seminole Indians are using boats, spears, and a special fence, called a weir, that was built across a river to channel and trap fish.

elder. The inedible bottle gourd was grown to make into containers, dippers, rattles, ladles, cups, bowls, and masks. By 1500 BCE, many Indians lived in small settlements made up of several dwellings and grew gardens of consumable plants.

As these early American Indians remained in the same villages for longer periods of time, they discovered ways to make their lives easier. Their farming methods—used to cultivate plants such as

This illustration shows a small settlement of Paleo-Indians. Their shelters are made from wooden stakes and animal hides.

corn, beans, and squash that were brought by traders from Central and South America—became more effective. They also refined the pottery that they made to store food.

As the Indians gained reliable sources of food and shelter, they became less dependent on moving from place to place to hunt and gather. This led to a growth in population, as well as the emergence of larger, more complex societies. Indeed, it is likely that different groups of Indians communicated and traded with each other.

When Europeans arrived in North America in the 1500s, they found sophisticated and complex Indian cultures that had taken thousands of years to develop. The Indians, like other groups in Asia and Africa encountering European explorers, tried to adapt to their new circumstances through negotiation, war, or a combination of the two.

ELEGANT FABRICS

Using plant fibers, animal fur, feathers, and natural vegetable dyes, the people of the Southeast United States produced fine, brilliantly colored textiles for hundreds, perhaps thousands, of years prior to the arrival of Europeans. While evidence of these fabrics is often scarce, Craig Mound at the Spiro site has yielded hundreds of delicate fragments. Study of these allows us to understand the sophisticated technologies used by the weavers.

When asked to imagine what people in the Southeast wore, most people today would think leather skirts and dresses, breechcloths, and moccasins. These would have been a part of their clothing, but people were also wearing and using large quantities of finely woven and decorated cloth, including bags to carry food and objects and mats to cover beds.

MEET BAST AND PAWPAW

The weavers used fiber, known as bast, from plants such as nettle, milkweed, and dogbane. These fibers are present in the thin outer layer of the stems of these plants and can be peeled off and processed, leaving fine, thin, white threads. Artisans were also processing the bark of certain trees, especially pawpaw. For thicker, more robust textiles, some weavers used the leaves of a plant known as rattlesnake master, while others, especially in the Gulf coastal areas, used Spanish moss. At Spiro, however, almost all the plant fiber textiles we see are from plants such as nettle or dogbane.

Spanish moss grows in long fibers, which lent themselves to being woven into fabrics.

LACE, GAUZE, AND MORE

The designs range from plain to extremely complex decorative weaves. Probably one of the most intriguing of the latter is a type referred to as "lace." Using careful manipulations of the warps, these textiles were woven using a combination of techniques. The overall result is a very fine, gauzy textile with bands of either circular openings or a "cross in circle" motif running through them.

Other examples of decorative textiles woven from plant fibers include twined textiles where the weaver has transposed or crossed the warps in order to create more open areas in the weave.

FINE RABBIT FUR

But people were not just using plant fibers. Animal fur, especially rabbit fur, was an important fiber source. At Spiro, we see multiple types of textiles made using spun rabbit fur. The cordage and thread spun from this would be similar to fine angora yarn produced today.

Not only were they spinning these threads of rabbit fur, but they were also dying them brilliant colors. Deep reds and bright yellows, as well as dark browns, deep black, and possibly even green, are common among Spiro textiles. In some cases, yarns were dyed first and then multiple colors used to twine textiles. In others, the textiles were woven first and then dyed, using a resist-dye technique such as batik or tie-dye.

BRIGHT DYES

In several of the Spiro textiles, we see evidence for geometric designs produced by using a resist-dye technique. Most likely, the textile would have been dyed a bright yellow first. Then, certain areas of the fabric would have been blocked off, by using a waxy substance or by tying threads around the cloth. The textile was then dyed again, this time producing a deep red. When the blocked-off areas were uncovered, the design would stand out against a deep red background.

Some of the examples we have of textiles where the yarns were dyed first and then used to weave a fabric are tiny fragments of extremely complex "tapestry twined" textiles. The size makes it very difficult to determine their use. Perhaps they were part of fairly large

Though this is not from the Spiro site, it is a good example of the patterns and colors that were woven into Native American textiles. This cotton fabric is from the Hohokam people, who settled in present-day Arizona.

robes, worn during ceremonies and dances; perhaps they were part of smaller garments, meant to be hung in temples. What is certain is that they were made using a hard, rigid fiber, possibly thin peels of cane, as the warps. Twined around them—horizontally, vertically, and even at an angle—are sequential lines of different colored spun and dyed rabbit fur threads.

By outlining blocks of color and weaving in different directions across the surface, weavers were able to create geometric designs and images of people and animals. These images are the same as those we see carved into marine shell cups and embossed into copper plates. Most likely, they represent important mythical characters or ancestors.

A GOOD USE FOR FEATHERS

Another version of these brilliantly dyed twined textiles is made with feather-wrapped cords. The use of feathers in textiles was common enough that scribes who accompanied the Spanish expeditions in the 1500s mention this practice specifically. In the fragments found at Spiro, we can see individual feathers wrapped around a vegetable fiber cord, with a second thinner cord used to help secure the feather. Changes in the colors of feathers down or up the length of these fragments indicate that this painstaking and highly skilled work would have been done as the textile was being woven. In this way, the weavers would have created blocks of color or other geometric designs across the surface of the textile. Analysis of the feathers indicates that most were from turkeys, swans, and geese. These feathers would have been dyed, in multiple colors, before being carefully wound around the vegetable-fiber warp cords.

BISON—WINTER AND SPRING

Another animal fur that the Spiroan weavers may have used is from bison. Among the textile finds at Spiro are rich, brownish-black bands of oblique interlacing. Bison fur is still used by Southeastern weavers to produce remarkably similar fabrics—long, but relatively narrow, bands, used as belts and garters. In the winter, bison produce a thick, extra layer of under-hair that is fine and soft. Collected in the spring when the bison molt, the fine soft fur would have easily produced the beautiful, dark, thin yarns we see in the bands of oblique interlacing. These, as well as the red-dyed textiles made from spun rabbit fur, were likely ritual regalia and worn by someone during a ceremony. These textiles were also used to make double-weave, decorated, river-cane baskets with lids.

Small textile fragments have been found at other sites—the Etowah Mounds in Georgia, for example. Imprints of textiles on ceramics from Wickcliffe, Kentucky, also offer fascinating glimpses into the rich tradition of fiber use and weaving among the people of the Southeast, as do European accounts of sixteenth- and seventeenth-century native textiles.

CHAPTER 3

ANCIENT MOUNDS

W
ho were the mound builders? When did they live? Why and how did they build such structures? When studying ancient or prehistoric cultures, questions such as those can be difficult to answer with any certainty because there is no written history. But decades of research provide some answers. Excavations help reveal some of the mysteries about the prehistoric people of North America.

Over the course of many centuries, several different Native American groups constructed mounds. Generally speaking, these eras are divided into three periods: the Archaic, the Woodland, and the Mississippian. For example, Louisiana's Watson Brake of 3500 BCE is believed to be the earliest known example of Archaic period mounds in the present-day United States. Around 1000 BCE, people of the Woodland period constructed conical burial earthworks, such as at Ohio's Marietta Earthworks. The last important mound-building culture was the Mississippian, and it is believed to have established itself by CE 800 and lasted until 1450—only a few decades before European contact.

Finds such as this falcon shaped from a metal called copper give archaeologists clues about the culture, resources, and technology of early people. This falcon from the Ohio Hopewell culture dates to between 200 and 100 BCE.

MISSISSIPPIAN SOCIETY

The Mississippian culture developed complex, hierarchical societies with an elite ruling class. The people were primarily farmers of corn, beans, squash, and other plants, but they also hunted, fished, and gathered wild foods including nuts and fruits. They traded with neighboring groups for wild game and other things they needed. While many people lived in small farming hamlets, some of the Mississippian cultures' permanent communities grew into large settlements.

The people probably came to the "big city" for special ceremonies, rituals, and to trade. The cities' locations, along the floodplains of the Mississippi River and along rivers in the southeastern portion of the United States, allowed the people to establish long-distance trading networks. They used local raw materials and exotic materials traded from distant places to make or adorn cups, bowls, smoking pipes, beads, and other ornaments to wear. Everyday items, including ceramic bowls and stone tools, were finely crafted. Ritual items, including stone pipes, shell cups, copper earspools, and copper plates depicting human and animal figures, were created by master artists.

WHAT WERE THE MOUNDS USED FOR?

Archaeologists have concluded that mounds of the Mississippian culture served both as tombs and as the foundation platforms for temples and chiefs' houses. The mounds exist in a variety of sizes. Some of them are quite large, requiring the coordinated labor of hundreds or thousands people. In a time well before the invention of any kind of vehicle and before Europeans introduced horses, mules, or oxen as beasts of burden, the mounds were built by hand with—literally—baskets of soil!

This photo shows one of the smaller mounds that sits atop Emerald Mound, near Natchez, Mississippi. Emerald Mound is one of the largest mounds in North America.

Some of the largest mounds of the Woodland era seem to have been used as tombs. After the death of an important member of the group, such as a warrior, elder, or religious leader, the body was placed in a pit or tomb made of logs. Sometimes the burial structure was burned and covered over with earth. When another person died, that person's body was added to the top of the original mound. Slowly, the mound increased in size and turned into a major hill of earth. Sometimes a saddle of land was made between two or more mounds to connect them.

Unlike the burial mounds built by earlier cultures, the Mississippian culture mounds were constructed as foundations for temples or chiefs' houses. They had a rectangular base with a series of flat tiers, or rows, at the top. At the death of each chief, the mound-top houses and temples were torn down and covered with a layer of earth. New buildings then were constructed for the new chief. Each time a level was added, the mound grew taller.

At the height of the Mississippian culture, around the years 1100 CE–1250 CE, hundreds of towns and settlements dotted the land along the major river systems of the eastern United States. Cahokia, in present-day Illinois, was critical to the culture's development. It was the largest indigenous city north of Mexico, and Monks Mound located there is the largest platform mound north of Mexico. The culture spread to the southeast, reaching Moundville in Alabama and Etowah in Georgia.

Monks Mound was built around 900 to 950 CE. It used to look different all those years ago, but precipitation and geological shifting have cause a great deal of slumping.

THE COMMUNITIES DECLINE

By 1400, however, many of the great ceremonial mound centers were in a decline. Archaeologists have tried to offer some ideas as to why the once-successful communities began to fail: the large populations of these native cultures may have depleted the soils and forests, thus reducing their food and building supplies. When bison—a reliable source of food, clothing, and shelter—started to appear in greater numbers, a nomadic lifestyle may have become more appealing. Some sites also show evidence of stockaded walls, indicating that the settlements were attempting to protect themselves from a threat of some kind.

Today, more than half the states in America contain ancient earthen mounds. Many of the mounds that survived through the centuries are protected in state and national parks. Most locations have museums and some reconstructed dwellings that display various artifacts and illustrate the lifestyles of America's ancient mound-building people.

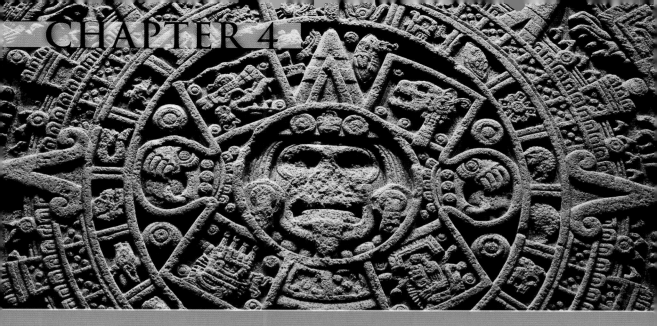

CHAPTER 4

NEXT STOP, MEXICO!

The people who first inhabited the Americas did not only settle in southeastern North America. They settled in all parts of the present-day United States, Canada, Mexico, and South America. Let's focus a little on the people who made their way south toward Mexico.

Mexico has had a long and colorful history. Just hearing the words Maya, Aztec, Quetzalcoatl, and Montezuma fills your head with pictures of battles, feathered headdresses, massive pyramids, and a jungle landscape.

This is a modern map of Mexico. Mexico's first people settled in various places, and their cultures became shaped by the landscape in which they found themselves.

Mexico's first inhabitants arrived forty thousand years ago. Originally hunters, they quickly settled down to a peaceful existence as farmers. Around 1200 BCE, the Olmec culture began to develop. Walking through dense jungle, it is quite a surprise to come across one of the immense carved heads that have survived to remind us of their existence.

The Mayan civilization, which developed on the Yucatan Peninsula, dominated from 300 BCE to 800 CE, and there are still Maya living today. They had a 365-day calendar and were successful architects, astronomers, and mathematicians; their pyramids are admired worldwide.

The Toltecs, who lived in central Mexico, built the city of Tollan, "place of the reeds," near the present city of Tula. Their leader, Topiltzin, introduced the cult of the plumed serpent Quetzalcoatl, the god of learning, and adopted his name. According to legend, Quetzalcoatl (the ruler) was a skilled farmer, and was light-skinned, longhaired, bearded, and peaceful. He hated warfare and human sacrifices practiced by other tribes. Forced out of Tula in 987, he burned everything behind him. Both Toltecs and Aztecs worshipped him, believing that when he left on a raft of snakes, he and would someday return.

The Aztec civilization reached its peak in the 1400s. Using force to hold their empire together, they overran the Toltec Empire. They built pyramids and developed a writing and number system. They were excellent artists, craftsmen, architects, city planners, engineers, astronomers, statesmen, warriors, and farmers. They had an advanced water management system composed of large canals, dykes to protect against floods, and man-made reservoirs to keep fresh water. Their exceptional agriculture methods included complex irrigation systems, the cultivation of swampland, and *chinampas*, small artificial islands built on freshwater lakes to grow crops.

Ruled by priests, the Aztecs worshipped many gods. Guided by their gods, the Aztecs searched for years for a place to settle. The sign that they had found it would be an eagle sitting on a cactus with a snake in its mouth. In 1325, they founded Tenochtitlan (tay-noke-TEET-laan), where presumably they saw such a sign on the site of what is now Mexico City. In 1502, Montezuma became their emperor. In 1519, with the arrival of the Spanish, the conquest of Mexico began. The Pre-Columbian civilization in the Americas was at and end.

This illustration shows Aztec warriors defending Tenochtitlan. When Spain took over, it eventually built Mexico City on the site of Tenochtitlan.

RECONSTRUCTING COPÁN

Copán was once a picturesque valley with about two thousand residents. People grew plenty of food in small, fertile pockets of alluvial soil along the Copán River. They also made pottery. Their native culture was different from Maya culture.

On the ninth of September in 426 CE (or 8.19.10.11.0 in the Maya long-count calendar), a Mayan warrior named Yax K'uk' Mo' and his group invaded Copán, changing it forever. He married a local woman of high rank, probably the daughter of the chief K'ak' Hun K'awil, and became the king. Bone chemistry shows that

Yax K'uk' Mo' lived his childhood and teen years in central Petén, modern Guatemala.

Winning Copán wasn't easy. Skeletal tests revealed that Yax K'uk' Mo' suffered many battle injuries—shattered bones in his right arm, damage to the skull and left shoulder. Yax K'uk' Mo' persisted and established the Copán dynasty. He started the construction of elaborate buildings, monuments, and hieroglyphs that made the Copán valley a part of the Maya culture. When Yax K'uk' Mo' died (at between fifty-five and seventy years of age), the Copán dynasty was well established. The pyramids, ball courts, stelae, and altars declared

This stela, or column, is in Copán, in Honduras. The stela is carved with a figure and other designs.

the histories and successful war campaigns of Copánec rulers. These structures also served to impress the local residents. The rule of the Copán dynasty was peaceful for four hundred years. The first tragedy that shook the family happened in Quirigua—about a three days' walk from Copán. Low-ranking elites (high-class citizens) with close links to the Copán royal family ruled Quirigua.

Waxakalajuun Ub'aah K'awiil, the thirteenth king of Copán, was sacrificed in Quirigua in 738 CE during a state visit. Scientists aren't sure if the act was a coup, but soon after Quirigua declared her independence from Copán. Anthropologist Dr. David Webster observes, "Nonroyal elites . . . really come into their own after the demise of Waxakalajuun, when the royal family lost much credibility."

Yax Pasaj (763–820 CE), the sixteenth ruler, came to power in a situation of bitter political rivalry between elite families. There were many powerful elite men but few political positions. The king couldn't oblige everyone. During his forty-seven-years rule, he built many impressive buildings. But the infighting among the elites continued. To complicate matters Yax Pasaj left no heir. The unrest spilled over, and a mob burned, looted, and destroyed Yax Pasaj's grave, funerary temple, council house, and monuments of royal line. The dynastic rule ended in 822 CE.

Why did people leave Copán? Analysis of skeletal remains shows that many of the elite were as weak and malnourished as the commoners. Getting enough food was a challenge for everyone. The macrofossils in soil samples confirm that many edible plants—maize (corn), beans, squash, bottle gourd, chayote, avocado, and possibly zapote—were grown in Copán. But, as the radiocarbon pathway of human skeletons shows, maize formed up to 78 percent of the diet for all ages, sexes, and social levels.

This detail from an altar created in 766 shows Yax K'uk' Mo', the founder of the dynasty that ruled Copán, passing the torch to Yax Pasaj, the last ruler. In all, the altar has sixteen leaders carved into it.

The workload made people weak and sick. Every job—the tilling of lands or carving the enormous monuments—required intense physical labor. Scientists estimate that a vaulted two-story-high building needed about 32,751 days to complete.

And food wasn't easy to come by. Anthropologist Dr. John Wingard calculated the agricultural production in Copán and concluded, "By [800 CE] at least 46.3 square miles [120 square km] of the best land in the valley had been colonized and deforested." The population continued to grow.

By 900 CE, the population was at its peak, at about 2,422 people per square mile. The worst mistake made was that the founders had unknowingly built the city center in the middle of the best farmland. To feed the growing population, farmers had to plant on the slopes. They also switched to a risky method of farming that stripped the soil. One rainy season, between the eighth and ninth centuries CE, homes and fields lay buried in massive landslides.

Despite these problems, the achievements of Copán priests or scientists are stunning. It was at Copán that the Maya discovered that planets rotate around the sun. The Copán scientists traced the revolution of the planet Venus accurately and predicted solar eclipses. Giant sundials, made by shadows of two stelae, helped priests determine the accurate dates for harvesting, burning the milpas (corn), and replanting.

Copán has many secrets. We are still discovering them.

THE GREAT PYRAMID OF CHOLULA

When most of us think about pyramids, we think of Egypt. But Central America is home to hundreds of these huge ancient structures. In fact, the Great Pyramid of Cholula in Mexico is the world's largest man-made monument by volume—4.45 million cubic meters. In contrast, the Great Pyramid of Egypt, the one that would have held Khufu's mummy, is a mere 2.6 million cubic meters in volume.

The ancient village of Cholula, located just west of present-day Puebla in Mexico, was founded more than two thousand years ago, making it possibly the oldest living city in the Americas. Its famous stepped pyramid was built and enlarged in several stages between 200

This hand-colored lithograph shows the pyramid at Cholula. You can see people and sheep on the hillsides surrounding the temple.

BCE and 900 CE. Many scholars believe that ancient peoples around the world built pyramids to be closer to their gods. The one at Cholula was dedicated to the powerful, feathered serpent god, Quetzalcoatl.

Over the centuries, Cholula grew in power and importance. By the time the Spanish arrived in Mexico in 1519, it was a major commercial and religious center. It housed more than 360 temples, was dominated by the Great Pyramid, and was second in importance only to the Aztec capital Tenochtitlan (present-day Mexico City) in population.

Today, Cholula's pyramid is a huge, tree-covered mound. On top sits an early Spanish church that still serves as a place of worship. During the twentieth century, archaeologists studied ancient Cholula. They excavated some 5 miles (8 km) of tunnels under the pyramid that tourists can explore. Among the finds was a 165-foot-long (50-meter-long) multicolored mural. The scenes show life-size figures participating in a religious ceremony.

CHAPTER 5

A LOOK AT THE INCA

I n the fifteenth century, a small tribe based in present-day Peru conquered about one hundred neighboring states and built a rich and sprawling empire with impressive cities and more than 14,000 miles (22,531 km) of roads. They accomplished all this without money or a written language!

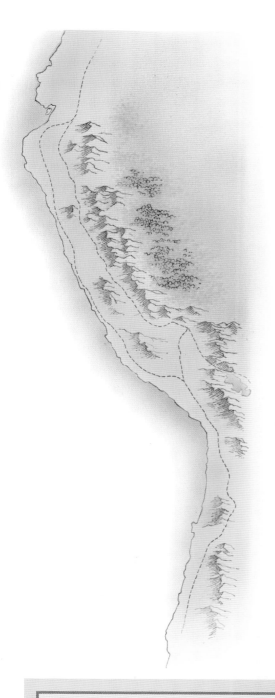

WORK AS CURRENCY

They divided captured lands into three shares: one for the state, one for the church, and one to feed the local population. Peasants farmed as usual, but the maize, potatoes, peanuts, and squash they grew belonged to the government. In turn, the government made sure everyone had enough to eat. The government also supplied clothing, but citizens spun and wove the fabric. Officials distributed cotton and llama wool and expected thread and cloth in return.

Inca rulers taxed their subjects in labor instead of money or crops. Each

This map shows the area along South America's coast where the Inca settled and created their empire.

HVAYNA
CCAPAC
INCA XII

household had to supply a worker for government service for a specific period of time. This system of mandatory public service was called mit'a, which translates as "rotation." Mit'a laborers served in the army, mined gold, quarried stone, built bridges, cared for the sick—whatever the state needed. Mit'a workers terraced the steep Andes mountainsides and constructed irrigation canals on the dry coastal plains.

FOOD SURPLUS HELPS STABILIZE THE ECONOMY

As food production became more sophisticated and stable, the government could store the surplus and allow some workers to specialize in the arts, including architecture, metalwork, and ceramics. Through the mit'a system, the state was able to move goods and provide services, and people from different parts of the empire came into contact with each other. No one person or region carried too heavy a burden since the most difficult jobs required the shortest rotation.

AYNI AND REWARDS

To prevent rebellion, especially in conquered areas, the Inca emphasized ayni. This "unofficial contract" encouraged those under Inca control to believe that if they worked for the state, the state

This painting (*left*) shows the Inca king Huayna Capac. Huayna Capac lived in the late 1400s and extended the Incan Empire a great deal, including conquering lands in Chile, Argentina, Ecuador, and Colombia.

Machu Picchu is nestled in the Andes in Peru to the northwest of Cuzco, and it is beautiful even in ruins today. It is thought it was built as the estate for Emperor Pachacuti around 1450.

would take care of them. In addition to providing seeds, tools, food, clothing, and medicine, the government located llama herds in villages that had never had them before and made sure that mit'a workers constructed religious monuments. The government also sponsored long festivals and supplied plenty of the corn beer known as chicha.

The Inca used additional rewards to keep local leaders content. The Inca system did not aim for equality: nobles could own personal land and skip mit'a labor. Rulers showered the loyal elite with gifts of land, jewelry, livestock, luxurious fabric, and even women. And, just in case, the Inca required the sons of high-ranking officials to attend school in the capital of Cuzco. These privileged students doubled as hostages.

EUROPEANS ARRIVE

For more than a century the empire had thrived without currency. However, the area's wealth excited Spanish conquistadors, who imagined how much money they could make by selling Inca gold back home in Europe. The military campaigns led by the Spanish conquistador Francisco Pizzaro, combined with the European diseases to which South Americans had no immunity, quickly destroyed the richest cashless empire in the world.

PRE-COLUMBIAN CIVILIZATION COMES TO AN END

The Pre-Columbian civilization encompasses thousands of years and many different groups of people. Each group was shaped by the place in which they settled. As these early people became more settled, their societies also became more advanced. This is evidenced by the complex structures they built and by the progress made in the development of tools. Thankfully, these early Americans left behind clues for archaeologists and other scientists to discover. Without them, we would not know about the rich cultures of these people before Europeans came and ultimately brought an end to the Pre-Columbian civilization.

CHRONOLOGY

40,000–13,000 years ago BCE People migrated from Asia into the Americas using the Bering land bridge.

10,000 BCE The first inhabitants of Mexico migrate into the Central Valley region.

c. 8000 BCE The climate in North America stabilizes and populations rise across the Americas.

c. 5000 BCE More advanced societies develop across the region.

c. 6500 BCE Complex mounds were built for ceremonies and religious reasons.

3500 BCE Watson Brake is built and continues to be added to over the next 500 years.

c. 2000 BCE Advanced Mesoamerican cultures develop.

1200 BCE–200 BCE The Olmecs dominate during an age called the pre-classical period.

1000 BCE–1000 CE The Woodland Period on the eastern coast of North America. There was a shift in the tools used and shelters built during this period.

300 BCE–800 CE Mayan culture thrives.

800–1450 CE The Mississippian culture takes hold in the Southeast and Midwest, but especially along the Mississippi and Ohio rivers.

1250–1519 CE Aztec culture prospers during the post-classical period.

1519 Spanish explorer Hernando Cortes lands in America. Two years later, the Aztec city of Tenochtitlan falls to the Spanish. By 1521, the Spanish have conquered all of central Mexico.

GLOSSARY

archaeologist A scientist who studies the past by digging ancient sites.

caribou Large reindeer.

chinampa A floating garden used by the Aztecs.

conical Shaped like a cone.

descendant A person who came from an ancestor.

earspool An earplug worn through a hole in the earlobe.

indigenous Originating in an area.

isthmus A stretch of land connecting two larger pieces of land.

mastodon An extinct mammal that resembles an elephant.

migrate To move from one place to another.

molt To shed old feathers, hair, or skin so new ones can grow

oblique interlacing A type of weaving where the warps meet the side edges at a diagonal, rather than the traditional right angle; also known as "finger-weaving."

Paleo A term that comes from the Greek word palaios, which means "ancient."

peat A substance made from decayed vegetable matter.

prehistoric Existing before written records.

sloth A slow-moving mammal that has long, hooklike claws it uses to hang upside down from trees.

warp One of the two basic types of threading used to make cloths. The warp goes over and under the weft, the other type of threading.

FURTHER READING

BOOKS

Edwards, Sue Bradford. *Ancient Maya.* Minneapolis, MN: Essential Library, 2015.

Joseph, Frank. *Unlocking the Prehistory of America.* New York, NY: Rosen, 2014.

Kenney, Karen. *Ancient Aztecs.* Minneapolis, MN: Essential Library, 2015

Levy, Janey. *North America's First People.* New York, NY: Gareth Stevens, 2017.

Murphy, John. *Gods and Goddesses of the Inca, Maya, and Aztec Civilizations.* New York, NY: Rosen, 2014.

WEBSITES

DK Find Out! Incas
www.dkfindout.com/us/history/incas/
Learn more about the Inca, including how they lived and what they ate.

Native American History, Pre-European Period
www.cabrillo.edu/~crsmith/anth7_hist1.html
Dive deeper into the history and cultures of Pre-Columbian America.

PBS, Lost King of the Maya
www.pbs.org/wgbh/nova/maya/
Tour the city of Copán, explore a map of the Mayan Empire, and decipher Mayan hieroglyphs.

INDEX